M000189871

ABINGDON SQUARE

WORKS BY MARIA IRENE FORNES

The Widow (1961)

Tango Place (1963) [originally titled *There! You Died!*]

The Successful Life of Three (1965)

Promenade (music by Al Carmines) (1965)

The Office (1966)

A Vietnamese Wedding (1967)

The Annunciation (1967)

Dr. Kheal (1968)

The Red Burning Light (1968)

Molly's Dream (1968)

The Curse of Langston House (1972)

Aurora (music by John Fitzgibbon) (1974)

Cap-a-pie (music by José Raul Bernando) (1975)

Washing (1976)

Fefu and Her Friends (1977)

Lolita in the Garden (music by Richard Weinstock) (1977)

In Service (1978)

Eyes on the Harem (1979)

Evelyn Brown (A Diary) (1980)

A Visit (music by George Quincy)

The Danube (1981)

Mud (1983)

Sarita (music by Leon Odenz) (1984)

No Time (1984)

Drowning (1985)

The Conduct of Life (1985)

Lovers and Keepers (music by Tito Puente and Fernando Rivas)

A Matter of Faith (1986)

The Mothers (1986)

Art (Box Plays) (1986)

Abingdon Square (1987)

What of the Night? (1988) [includes *Nadine* (1986);
Springtime (1988); *Lust* (1988); and *Hunger* (1988)]

Oscar and Bertha (1991)

Terra Incognita (opera, music by Roberto Sierra) (1991)

Enter the Night (1993)

Ibsen and the Actress (1995)

Manual for the Desperate Crossing (later *Balseros/Rafters*)
(libretto for an opera by Robert Ashley) (1996)

The Summer in Gossensass (1997)

ABINGDON SQUARE

∾

Maria Irene Fornes

GREEN INTEGER
KØBENHAVN · LOS ANGELES
2000

GREEN INTEGER BOOKS
Edited by Per Bregne
København/Los Angeles

Distributed in the United States by Consortium Book
Sales and Distribution, 1045 Westgate Drive, Suite 90
Saint Paul, Minnesota 55114-1065
and in England and the Continent by
Central Books
99 Wallis Road, London E9 5LN
(323) 857-1115/http://www.greeninteger.com

First Edition 2000
©2000 by Maria Irene Fornes
Published by agreement with Helen Merrill Ltd.

This book was published in collaboration with
The Contemporary Arts Educational Project, Inc.,
a non-profit corporation, through a matching grant from the
National Endowment for the Arts, a federal Agency.

NATIONAL
ENDOWMENT
FOR THE
A R T S

Design: Per Bregne
Typography: Guy Bennett
Cover: Photograph by Marcella Scuderi

ABOUT THE PLAY

An earlier version of *Abingdon Square* was given a workshop production at Seattle Repertory Theatre in 1984. Following a staged reading at New York's American Place Theatre in April, *Abingdon Square* opened there on October 8, 1987, produced by the Women's Project and Productions Inc. and directed by the author. The text published here is a revision completed by the author in 1992.

CHARACTERS

MARION, *from age 15 to 24.*
JUSTER, MARION's *husband, from age 50 to 59.*
MICHAEL, JUSTER's *son, the same age as Marion.*
FRANK, MARION's *lover, one year older than* MARION.
MARY, MARION's *cousin, the same age as* MARION.
MINNIE, MARION's *great-aunt, from age 58 to 67.*
THE GLAZIER, *a very strong, playful man.*
THOMAS, MARION's *son, eight months old.*

TIME AND PLACE

Act One: 1908–1912. In a house on 10th Street, New York City.
Act Two: 1915–1917. In the house on 10th Street, Mary's place, an apartment on Abingdon Square, a beer parlor, and Minnie's house.

SETTINGS

The living room of a house on 10th Street. To the right is a double door which leads to the foyer and the main door. On the back wall there are two large French doors. On the right there are double doors that lead to other rooms. Up center, a few feet from the back wall are a sofa and two armchairs. On each side of the sofa there is a tall stand with a vase. Down left there are a chess table and two side chairs; down right there is a small desk. There is a chair on the upstage side of the desk and another on the right side. During intermission a telephone is placed on the desk.

The attic room or closet. A platform about two feet high on the left side of the stage. On the back wall there is a small door.

MARY's *living room. An embroidered shawl is placed on the sofa.*

The living room of an apartment on Abingdon Square. A back wall is placed behind the sofa. On the wall there is a fireplace; above the fireplace there is a large mirror.

The beer parlor. A square plain wood table and two chairs in a pool of red light, center stage.

MINNIE's *living room. A chair center stage in a pool of light.*

JUSTER's *bedroom. A platform about two feet high on the right side of the stage. On the back wall there is a small door. Parallel to the back wall there is a narrow bed.*

ACT ONE

SCENE 1: *10th Street. August, 1908. It is dusk.*
JUSTER *sits in the garden facing up left. He sings*
Handel's "Where'er You Walk." MARION *hides*
between the two windows and listens.

JUSTER: [*Singing*] Where'er you walk,
Cool gales shall fan the glades.

> *She moves to the left window and looks at him.*

Trees, where you sit
Shall crowd into a shade. Trees, where you sit,
Shall crowd into a shade.

MARION: Pst!

> JUSTER *leans over to see who has called.*
> MARION *moves her hand towards him.*

SCENE 2: *Two weeks later. It is a sunny afternoon.*
MARION *enters running from the left.* MICHAEL
is chasing her. They run around the room laugh-
ing and screaming. He grabs her and takes a piece
of chocolate from her hand. He unwraps the choco-
late and puts it in his mouth. She chases him. She
grabs him and they fall. He covers his mouth. She
tries to pull his hand away.

MARION: Give it to me.

> *He swallows the chocolate, lets her remove his hand, and opens his mouth.*

MICHAEL: It's gone. I swallowed it.

MARION: You're bad! [*She holds him tightly*] I love you Mike! I love you.

> *He holds her.*

MICHAEL: Me too! I love you too!

MARION: You are like a brother to me. I love you as a sister loves a brother. But I must love you as a mother. I must be a mother to you. You need a mother. How could a boy like you grow up without a mother. You need a mother.

MICHAEL: You're more to me than any mother could ever be. You're my sister, my daughter, my cousin, my friend. You are my friend! My grandmother!

MARION: You're joking and I'm serious.

MICHAEL: I'm serious. You are to me the best person I'll ever know. The best person I will ever know.

MARION: [*Standing*] You need a guide, a teacher in life.

MICHAEL: I don't need a guide.

MARION: You need someone who'll tell you what to do.

MICHAEL: I don't. I'm doing fine. I'm a good boy. My mother would say to me, "You're doing fine m'boy.

You give me no trouble and you don't need a mother." When I need help I'll go to my best friend, who is you.

As the following speech progresses MARION *speaks rapidly as if in an emotional trance.*

MARION: You're sweet. You are the sweetest creature on earth. I wish I were sweet like you. I wish I had sweetness in my heart the way you do. Soon I will, officially, be your mother, and I say this in earnest, I hope I can make myself worthy of both you and your father. He brought solace to me when I knew nothing but grief. I experienced joy only when he was with me. His kindness brought me back to life. I am grateful to him and I love him. I would have died had he not come to save me. I love him more than my own life and I owe it to him. And I love you because you are his son, and you have a sweetness the same as his. I hope I can make myself worthy of the love you have both bestowed upon me and I hope to be worthy of the honor of being asked to be one of this household which is blessed—with a noble and pure spirit. I'm honored to be invited to share this with you and I hope that I succeed in being as noble of spirit as those who invite me to share it with them. I know I sound very formal, and that my words seem studied. But there is no

9

other way I can express what I feel. In this house light comes through the windows as if it delights in entering. I feel the same. I delight in entering here and when I'm not here I feel sad. I delight in walking through these rooms and I'm sad when I leave. I cannot wait for the day when my eyes open from a night's sleep and I find myself inside these walls. Being here I feel as if I'm blessed. If life dealt me a cruel blow when my parents died, now it offers me the kindest reward. I hope I never give either of you cause to regret having invited me to share both your lives. I hope you, as well as he, will always tell me if I have done something wrong—or if you have any reason for disappointment. Would you promise me you will?

MICHAEL: I promise.

SCENE 3: *A few minutes later.* MINNIE *and* JUSTER *are entering from the foyer.* MARION *stands left.*

MINNIE: [*As she goes to sit, to* MARION] Sit down, dear.
    MINNIE *sits right.* JUSTER *sits left.* MARION *sits on the sofa.*

MINNIE: I was just talking to Juster about the question of your obligations. The questions you posed to me, and whether you will continue your studies, or what obligations you will have. And we thought you should ask the questions directly to him. The questions you asked me. He doesn't seem to know the answer. Go ahead dear.

MARION: I wanted to know about my obligations here. I believe that when one marries one has obligations and I asked Aunt Minnie what those obligations would be. And she said she was not sure. But that she thought maybe I will be running the house. Is that so? And I told her that I have never run a house and I don't know if it's something I could learn to do. I told her that I should tell you that I have never run a house. It may be that you don't feel I am suited to do it.

JUSTER: I'm embarrassed to say that I have no idea how to run the house. When I was born my mother ran the house. Then when I married my wife, Martha ran it. Then, when she became ill, Jenny, our housekeeper, took over the running of the house. And when my wife Martha died, Jenny continued running the house till now. I never did.

MARION: And what does running a house consist of?

JUSTER: I don't know, Marion. Minnie, don't you know?

MINNIE: Yes, I do. I run my own house, Juster. But I don't know if you run your house the same way I run mine.

JUSTER: You should talk to Jenny, Marion, and decide what it is you want to do.

MARION: Thank you, I will. Will my cousin Mary continue giving me instructions? I would like to know if that is something I will continue doing—if she will continue tutoring me.

JUSTER: Indeed Marion, nothing in your life should change unless you want it to.

MARION: Because of all the years I was not able to go to school I feel I don't yet comprehend a great many things.

SCENE 4: *Two months later, October, 1908. It is dusk.* JUSTER *stands center left.* MICHAEL *stands up left.* MARY *stands up right.* MARION *and* MINNIE *embrace center.* MARION *holds a white veil and a missal.* MINNIE *sobs.*

MARION: My dear aunt. I am happy. Believe me, I am happy. I will be very happy.

MINNIE *sobs.* MARION *holds her. A few seconds pass.*

MARION: Don't cry, my dear.

MINNIE *sobs.* MARION *holds her. A few seconds pass.*

MARION: My dear aunt, don't cry.

MINNIE *goes on sobbing.* MARION *releases*

her slowly and takes a step away from her, MARION *lowers her head.* MARY *puts her arm around* MINNIE *and exits with her.* MINNIE *mumbles and cries while she exits.*

MARION: Why is she so unhappy?

JUSTER: Weddings make people cry, Marion.

      MARION *looks at him.* JUSTER *takes her hand and brings it to his lips. She kisses his cheek.*

SCENE 5: *Six months later. April, 1909. It is late afternoon.* MARION *sits at the desk. She writes in a notebook. There is an open textbook in front of her.* MARY *is standing next to her, leaning over. There is a short exchange of conspiratorial whispering, ear to ear.*

MARY: That's what I heard.

MARION: Who told you!

MARY: My cousin. He knows his family—him and his family. And her and her sister. He also knows him—the man is married. And the wife's sister came to visit. She lives in New Palz and her sister, the wife, is also from New Palz. They're both from New Palz—his wife and his wife's sister. The sister came to visit and she stayed for months. The three of them slept together. Together in the same bed. The man and the wife and the wife's sister slept together in the same bed.

MARION: The three of them?

MARY: Yes! The three of them in the same bed.

MARION: Why did they do that?

MARY: To make love!

MARION: How?

MARY: I don't know. I imagine he first makes love to one and then the other.

Both squeal, terrified and thrilled.

MARION: That's perverse!

MARY: That's why I'm telling you.

MARION: It's horrendous!

MARY: I know.

MARION: How did you find out?

MARY: He told me.

MARION: He!

MARY: My cousin.

MARION: How did he know?

MARY: Everyone knows.

MARION: How?

MARY: Noises in the bedroom. The servant heard them.

MARION: It couldn't be true.

MARY: Oh yes, if you see them you would know.

MARION: How?

MARY: The way they look at each other.

MARION: How?

MARY: Obscenely, Marion, and sexually.

MARION: The wife is not jealous?

MARY: No.

MARION: And the sister is not jealous?

MARY: No.

MARION: He looks at them both?

MARY: Yes!

MARION: In the street?

MARY: Yes. He looks at one and then the other—passionately.

MARION: He's shameless.

MARY: The three of them are.

MARION: It's he who does it.

MARY: They too. They also look at him.

MARION: With passion?

MARY: Yes.

MARION: In front of the other?

MARY: They don't mind.

MARION: They don't?

MARY: Apparently not.

MARION: Then, the wife's to blame.

MARY: Yes, it's her fault, not his.

MARION: It's his fault, too.

MARY: The sister is pretty. Who can blame him?

MARION: She is?

MARY: Yes. If she lets him—what is he to do?

MARION: He can say no.

MARY: If the wife doesn't mind why should he?

MARION: Because it's sinful. It's a sin he commits. He will go to hell. God won't forgive him. It's his soul. He can't just say, "They don't mind." He should mind. It is his own soul he has to save. He'll go to hell.

MARY: I know. They'll all go to hell.

MARION: And so will we.

MARY: We?

MARION: For talking about it!

MARY: No, we won't!

MARION: Yes! Because we talked about it, we'll go to hell.

MARY: We didn't do anything!

MARION: Yes, we did!

MARY: What!

MARION: We talked about it and we thought about it.

MARY: Did you!

MARION: Yes.

MARY: What did you think?

MARION: I thought about it. I imagined everything!

MARY: Marion, how could you?

MARION: Didn't you?

MARY: No!

MARION: Oh, God! I've sinned!

MARY: Oh, Marion! Repent.

MARION: I repent! Oh God! I repent! Oh God! How could I? Oh God! [*She falls on her knees. She is out of breath*] Oh, God! Forgive me! [*She begins to calm down*]

MARY: [*Kneeling next to her*] What did you think?

MARION: The three of them in bed.

MARY: What did they do?

MARION: I can't tell you.

MARY: What.

MARION: He makes love to one while the other is there, very close. She looks and she listens. She watches their bodies move. What they say. She's very close.

MARY: How close?

MARION: Touching. She must.

MARY: That's just awful.

MARION: It must be.

MARY: Oh, Marion. And then?

MARION: He kisses her.

MARY: Which one.

MARION: The other one.

MARY: No!

MARION: He holds them both. And knows them both.

      MARY gasps.

MARY: Oh, Marion. I too have sinned. Will God forgive us?

      They embrace.

SCENE 6: *One month later. May, 1909. It is evening.* JUSTER *sits up left reading.* MICHAEL *sits cross-legged on the floor in front of the sofa. He reads a book.* MARION *sits at the desk. She writes in a diary. The lights are dim except where Juster sits.*

JUSTER: [*Reading**]: If you wish to see it for yourself, take a pencil and push the pointed end into the open mouth of the flower and downward toward the ovary and the honey, just as a bee would thrust in its tongue. If it is a young flower you have chosen you will see the two anthers bend down as if they knew what they were doing, and touch the pencil about two inches from the point leaving a smudge of golden pollen on it. A day later, the stigma will have lengthened and, if you would, then push your pencil in again. You will find that it now hangs far enough to touch the pencil in the same place where the pollen was laid, while the empty anthers have shriveled. Thus on its first day of opening the anthers rub their pollen on the back of visiting bees; and on the next the stigma hangs down far enough to receive pollen from a younger flower. If you wish to see the mechanism by which the anthers are bent

---

* From *My Garden in Autumn and Winter* by E. A. Bowles.

down, cut away the hood until you lay bare the stamens as far as the point where they are joined to the corolla. Here you will notice that they have slender white flying buttresses that keep them in place. Just in front, standing in the tube of the flower, are two white levers growing out from the filaments and blocking the mouth of the tube. Push your pencil in again and you can see what happens. It strikes against the levers and pushes them down with it. As the buttresses hold the filaments in place, their upper portion is bent over from that point until the anthers touch the pencil.

SCENE 7: *The attic. Five months later. October, 1909. It is morning.* MARION *stands on her toes with her arms outstretched, looking upward. She wears a white camisole and underskirt. Her whole body shakes with strain. She perspires heavily. On the floor there is a blanket and a large open book. She rapidly recites the following passage from Dante's "Purgatorio."* MINNIE's *words should not interrupt* MARION's *speech.*

MARION†: He girt me in such manner as had pleased
Him who instructed; and O strange to tell

† From the 19th-century translation by Henry Frances Cary.

As he selected every humble plant,
Wherever one was pluck'd another there
Resembling, straightway in its place arose.
Canto II: They behold a vessel under
conduct of an angel.
Now had the sun to that horizon reach'd,
That covers with the most exalted point
Of its meridian circle, Salem's walls;
And night, that opposite to him her orb
Rounds, from the stream of Ganges issued forth
Holding the scales, that from her hands are dropt
When she reigns highest: so that where I was
Aurora's white and vermeil-tinctured cheek
To orange turn'd as she in age increased.
Meanwhile we linger'd by the water's brink,
Like men, who, musing on their road, in thought
Journey, while motionless the body rests.
When lo! as, near upon the hour of dawn,
Through the thick vapors Mars with fiery beam
Glares down in west, over the ocean floor;

MINNIE: [*Offstage*] Marion…

MARION: So seem'd, what once again I hope to view,
A light, so swiftly coming through the sea,
No winged course might equal its career.
From which when for a space I had withdrawn

Mine eyes, to make inquiry of my guide,
Again I look'd, and saw it grown in size

MINNIE: [*Offstage*] Marion…

MARION: And brightness: then on either side appear'd
Something, but what I knew not, of bright hue
And by degrees from underneath it came
Another. My preceptor silent yet
Stood, while the brightness, that we first discern'd
Open'd the form of wings: then when he knew

MINNIE [*Offstage*] Marion, are you there?

MARION: The pilot, cried aloud, "Down, down; bend low
Thy knees; behold God's angel: fold thy hands:
Now shalt thou see true ministers indeed." [*She faints*]

MINNIE: [*Offstage*] Marion, are you there? …[*A moment passes*] Marion…

MARION: [*Coming to*]…Yes. Don't come up…I'll be right down.

    MINNIE *enters.*

MINNIE: Are you all right?

MARION: …Yes.

MINNIE: [*Kneeling and holding* MARION *in her arms*] What are you doing?

MARION: I'm studying.

MINNIE: …You're drenched…

MARION: I know…

MINNIE: Why don't you study where it's cool?

MARION: I have to do it here.

MINNIE: You look so white. [*Drying* MARION's *per-spiration*] Look at how you are drenched. Why do you do this?

MARION: I wasn't aware of the heat.

MINNIE: Now you are cold. You are as cold as ice.

> MARION *moves to the left. She leans against the wall and covers herself with the blanket.*

MARION: I feel sometimes that I am drowning in vagueness—that I have no character. I feel I don't know who I am. Mother deemed a person worthless if he didn't know his mind, if he didn't know who he was and what he wanted and why he wanted it, and if he didn't say what he wanted and speak clearly and firmly. She always said, "A person must know what he ought to believe, what he ought to desire, what he ought to do." I write letters to her. I know she's dead. But I still write to her. I write to her when I am confused about something. I write and I write until my thoughts become clear. I want my thoughts to be clear so she'll smile at me. I come to this room to study. I stand on my toes with my arms extended and I memorize the words till I collapse. I do this to strengthen my mind and my body. I am trying to conquer this vagueness I have inside of me. This lack of character. This numbness. This weakness—I have inside of me.

SCENE 8: *A day later. Dusk.* JUSTER *walks from left to right in the garden. He wears a shirt with the sleeves rolled up. He carries a small tree, whose roots are wrapped in canvas, under his arm.*

SCENE 9: *Five months later. March, 1910. It is late afternoon. There is a phonograph on the table.* MICHAEL *is placing the needle on a record. It plays a rag.* MARION *and* MICHAEL *dance.*

MICHAEL: That's it. That's it. Good. You're doing well. Ta rah. Pa rah.

MARION: Ta rah. Pa rah. Ta rah. Pa rah.

They make these sounds through the whole song. The record comes to an end.

MARION: Again…let's do it again. [*He starts the record again. They do the dance and sing again.*]

JUSTER *appears in the vestibule. He hangs his hat on the hatrack. He takes off his coat and hangs it in the closet. He comes into the living room and watches them dance.* MARION *sees* JUSTER *and waves to him. He waves to her.*

MARION: Look at me, I'm dancing. Look at this.
> *They do a special step.* JUSTER *smiles.*

MICHAEL: And this. [*He demonstrates another step*]

JUSTER: That's wonderful.

MICHAEL: Come, learn how to do it, Father.

JUSTER: [*Smiling*] Oh, I don't think I could.

MICHAEL: Yes, yes, you could. I'll teach you. I just taught Marion.

MARION: Oh, yes, it's easy. You just listen to the music and you immediately start dancing. I learned. You could learn too. I never thought I could learn and I did. Sing the words, "Tah rah. Pa rah. Tah rah. Pa rah."
> MARION *dances toward* JUSTER.

ALL THREE: [*Singing*] Tah rah. Pa rah. Tah rah. Pa rah.
> MICHAEL *puts* JUSTER'S *arms around* MARION *in dancing position. The* THREE *dance and sing.*

MICHAEL: Do it! Do it!

JUSTER *takes a couple of steps.*

JUSTER: Oh, I don't think I can. I never was light on my feet.

MICHAEL: Yes you are, Father. You could do it. You could dance beautifully. You already have the stance.

JUSTER: No, no, I'm sure I can't.

MARION: Do it again. You did it well.

JUSTER: I don't think so. You dance. [*Going to a chair*] I'll watch you from here. I like to watch you dance.

JUSTER *smiles and claps while they dance.*

SCENE 10: *Four months later. July, 1910. It is late afternoon.* MARION *sits at the desk. She is writing in a diary.* MICHAEL *appears in the doorway to the left. He holds flowers in his hand. He watches her. He tiptoes up behind her and covers her eyes.*

MARION: [*Pressing the diary against her chest*] Oh!

MICHAEL: [*Taking his hand away*] I didn't mean to scare you. It's only me. I brought you flowers.

MARION *gives a sigh of relief. She closes her diary.*

MICHAEL: Don't worry. I didn't read any of it.

MARION: It's a diary. [MICHAEL *sits*] I was describing an event.

MICHAEL: What event? Is it a secret?

MARION: It's a secret. A meeting.

MICHAEL: What sort of meeting?

MARION: Something imagined. In my mind.

MICHAEL: Diaries are to write things that are true.

MARION: Not this one. This diary is to write things that are not true. Things that are imagined. Each day I write things that are imagined.

MICHAEL: [*Reaching for the diary.*] Could I read it?

MARION: No.

MICHAEL: Why not? If it's things you imagined.

MARION: It would embarrass me.

MICHAEL: Is it romantic?

MARION: Yes. It is the story of a love affair.

MICHAEL: Whose?

MARION: A young man's named F.

MICHAEL: With whom?

MARION: With a young girl.

MICHAEL: What's her name?

MARION: M.

MICHAEL: Who is she?

MARION: Me!

MICHAEL: You!

MARION: Yes!

> *He gasps.*

MICHAEL: You! [*Touching the diary*] In a romance?

MARION: [*Taking the diary away from him*] Yes .

MICHAEL: How thrilling! —Do you write each day?

MARION: Yes.

MICHAEL: Since when?

MARION: Since August.

MICHAEL: Do you see him each day?

MARION: No.

MICHAEL: Why not?

MARION: Because I can't.

MICHAEL: Why not?

MARION: I'm married!

    MICHAEL laughs.

MICHAEL: Why are you married?

MARION: Because I am.

MICHAEL: If it's imagined, you don't have to be.

MARION: [*Righteous*] I couldn't do that.

MICHAEL: [*Laughing*] You're crazy.

MARION: A married woman could not do that.

    She opens her mouth in amazement and they laugh.

MICHAEL: Where do you meet?

MARION: In the street. In a parlor.

MICHAEL: Does he come here?

MARION: Here!

    He nods.

  …No!

MICHAEL: Go on.

MARION: We talk.

MICHAEL: Have you kissed?

MARION: No!

MICHAEL: Will you kiss him?

MARION: I think so. In the future.

MICHAEL: Is he real?

MARION: He is real, as real as someone who exists. I know every part of him. I know his fingernails— every lock of his hair.

MICHAEL: What does F stand for?

MARION: I haven't found out yet. Francis of course. What other name starts with an F?

MICHAEL: Franklin.

MARION: [*Laughing*] No. His name is not Franklin.

MICHAEL: Of course not. Floyd.

MARION: [*Still laughing*] No.

MICHAEL: Felix.

MARION: [*Still amused*] No. Don't say such things.

MICHAEL: I'm sorry.

MARION: Be discreet. You have to know how to enter another person's life.

MICHAEL: I know. I'm sorry. What does he look like? May I ask that?

MARION: He's handsome. He has a delicate face and delicate hands. His eyes are dark and his hair is dark. He looks like a poet. He looks the way poets look. Soulful.

MICHAEL: Where did you first meet him?

MARION: In a shop.

MICHAEL: And you talked?

MARION: Yes.

MICHAEL: Where does he live?

MARION: I don't know yet. I don't know him that well.

MICHAEL: How long have you known him?

MARION: Three months.

MICHAEL: That long?

MARION: Yes.

MICHAEL: How often do you meet?

MARION: Once a week.

MICHAEL: Why not more often?

MARION: You have to be careful.

MICHAEL: Why?

MARION: Because I'm married.

They laugh.

MICHAEL: You're mad.

She laughs.

MARION: I know.

SCENE 11: *Three months later. October 1910. It is morning.* MARION *enters right, carrying a hooded cloak. She walks left furtively and looks around. She puts on the cloak lifting the hood over her head, covering her face. She looks around again and exits right hurriedly.*

SCENE 12: *Three months later. January, 1911. It is evening. It is* JUSTER's *birthday.* MARION *sits in the chair to the* SR, MINNIE *and* MARY *stand by her side.* MICHAEL *sits on the floor to* MARION's *right. He holds a ukulele.* JUSTER *sits in the chair to the left.*

MARION: My dear husband, in honor of your birthday, we who are your devoted friends, son and wife, have prepared a small offering—an entertainment. May this, your birthday, be as happy an occasion for you as it is for us.

> MARION *extends her hand toward* MICHAEL, *who starts playing.*

MARION, MINNIE, MARY *and* MICHAEL: [*Singing**]:
True love never does run smooth
At least that's what I'm told,
If that is true then our love surely must be good as gold.
How we battle every day and when I want a kiss,
I have to start explaining
And it sounds about like this:
"Dearie, please don't be angry
'Cause I was only teasing you.
I wouldn't even let you think of leavin'
Don't you know I love you true.

Just because I took a look at somebody else
That's no reason you should put poor me on the shelf.
Dearie, please don't be angry
'Cause I was only teasing you."

* "Angry" by Dudley Mecum, Jules Cassard, Henry Brunies and Merrit Brunies.

They repeat the song. MARION *and* MARY *do a dance they have choreographed.*

MARION: Dear husband, now it's your turn to sing.

They all gesture toward JUSTER.

JUSTER: [*Singing*] "Dearie, please don't be angry
'Cause I was only teasing you.
I wouldn't even let you think of leavin'
Don't you know I love you true.

Just because I took a look at somebody else
That's no reason you should put poor me on the shelf.
Dearie, please don't be angry
'Cause I was only teasing you."

MARION *kisses* JUSTER *on the cheek.*

SCENE 13: *One month later. February, 1911. It is evening.* MARION *sits in the left chair.* MICHAEL *lies on the floor. They are both in a somber mood.*

MARION: It was he. There was no doubt in my mind. I saw him and I knew it was he.

MICHAEL: Did he see you?

MARION: No, I hid behind the stacks.

MICHAEL: Then?

MARION: I took a book and buried my head in it. I was afraid. I thought if he saw me he would know and I would die. He didn't. I saw him leave. For a

31

moment I was relieved he hadn't seen me and I stayed behind the stacks. But then I was afraid I'd lose him. I went to the front and I watched him walk away through the glass windows. Then, I followed him…a while…but then I lost him because I didn't want to get too near him. I went back there each day. To the bookstore and to the place where I had lost him. A few days later I saw him again and I followed him. Each time I saw him I followed him. I stood in corners and in doorways until I saw him pass. Then I followed him. I was cautious but he became aware of me. One day he turned a corner and I hurried behind him for fear of losing him. He was there, around the corner, waiting for me. I screamed and he laughed. He grabbed me by the arm. And I ran. I ran desperately. I saw an open entranceway to a basement and I ran in. I hid there till it was dark. Not till then did I dare come out. I thought perhaps he was waiting for me. When I saw that he wasn't there I came home. I haven't been outside since then. I'll never go out again, not even to the corner. I don't want to see him. I don't want him to see me. I'm ashamed of myself. I'm a worthless person. I don't know how I could have done what I did. I have to do penance.

SCENE 14: *Two months later. April, 1911. It is afternoon.* MARION *stands at the right window looking out.* JUSTER *is outside. There is a sound of shoveling as* JUSTER *speaks.*

JUSTER: Have you seen the Chinese Holly? It's already budding. It's the first to sprout. It's so eager for spring. Have you noticed how it's grown? It's less than two seasons that I planted it and look how tall it is now. [*Pause*] Marion—what are you looking at? It's this one I'm talking about. This one here, Marion.
    She walks to the window on the left.

MARION: Yes, it is tall.

SCENE 15: *Ten months later. February, 1912. It is evening.* MICHAEL *and* JUSTER *play chess at the table to the left.* MICHAEL *sits to the left.* JUSTER *stands behind* MICHAEL. *They both study the board.* MARION *stands up left.* JUSTER *turns to look at her.*

JUSTER: You look beautiful. You look like a painting. [*She smiles sadly.* JUSTER *turns to* MICHAEL.] Play, Michael. Make up your mind.

MICHAEL: I don't know what move to make.

JUSTER: Make whatever move seems best to you.

MICHAEL: I get confused. I don't see one move being better than the next.

JUSTER: What do you think, Marion?

MARION: What do I think?

JUSTER: Yes, what should Mike do? Should he scrutinize the board and imagine each move and its consequences, or should he just play and see what happens? I imagine both are good ways of learning. [*As he walks to center*] One way, I think, is a more Oriental way of learning—through meditation. The other is more Western. Reckless. We are reckless, we Westerners. Orientals meditate until they have arrived at a conclusion. Then they act. We Westerners act. Then, we look to see if what we did makes any sense. Which do you think is the best way to act?

MARION: I don't know. I think I'm like an Oriental. I don't think I take chances. I don't take any risks. I don't make any moves at all.

MICHAEL: [*As he moves a piece*] Check.

JUSTER *looks at the board.*

MARION: Does that mean you won?

MICHAEL: I don't know. [*He looks at* JUSTER. JUSTER *looks at him and smiles.*] It's exciting to check though. It's exciting to make a move and be reckless and create an upheaval. And for a moment to think that it's mate. [*To* JUSTER] Is it?

JUSTER: [*Making a move*] For now you just lose a bishop.

MARION: Maybe it's best to be like an Oriental.

MICHAEL: I don't know. When you reflect you have to know what you are reflecting about. When you move without reflecting [*as he moves a piece,* MARION *lifts her skirt to see her toes*] you just move. You just do it.
She takes six steps looking at her feet.

MARION: Six steps and the sky did not fall.

SCENE 16: *Seven months later. September, 1912. It is late afternoon. There are some letters on the chess table.* MARION *sits in a chair facing the window.* FRANK *stands in the garden outside the window.* MARION'S *manner of speaking reveals sexual excitement.*

MARION: You're trespassing. Where you are standing is private property. It's a private garden and when strangers come into it we let the dogs out.

FRANK: Let them tear me up. I'll stay here and look at you.
MARION *moves between the two windows.* FRANK *walks into the living room. She moves to the stage left chair and sits.* FRANK *follows her and sits at her feet. She starts to go. He grabs her ankle.*

MARION: Let go.

FRANK: I'm chained to you. I'm your shackle.

MARION: You are?

FRANK: [*Pulling her foot toward him*] Come.

35

MARION: [*Pulling back*] No. Let go.

FRANK: Never. [*She jerks her foot*] Never. [*She jerks her foot*] Never. [*She jerks her foot*] Never.

> *She laughs.*

MARION: What if someone sees you?

FRANK: I'll be arrested.

MARION: Let go of my foot. [*She touches his face. She is scared by her own action and withdraws her hand*]

FRANK: I know every move you make. I've been watching you. You spy on me and I spy on you.

MARION: Let go. Someone will see you.

FRANK: There's no one here to see us.

MARION: How do you know?

FRANK: He won't be home for hours.

MARION: Who?

FRANK: Your father.

> MARION *is startled by his remark and becomes somber. She walks to the chair next to the desk.*

MARION: He's not my father.

FRANK: Who is he?

MARION: He's my husband. [*They are silent a moment*] He is my husband and I don't want to see you ever again. I am married and you should not be here. [*Short pause*] Leave now, please.

> FRANK *is motionless for a moment. Then, he walks away.* JUSTER *enters. He opens the closet*

*in the foyer puts his hat and cane in it, closes the
door and walks into the living room. She is calm
and absent as if something had just died inside
her. She sits.* JUSTER *enters right.*

JUSTER: Good evening, dear.

MARION: Good evening.

     JUSTER *walks left, picks up the mail and looks
through it. He looks at her.*

JUSTER: Are you all right…? You look pale.

MARION: Do I look pale?

     He comes closer to her.

JUSTER: I think you do.

MARION: I'm fine.

     *He kisses her and walks left. He speaks with-
out turning.*

JUSTER: Is Michael home?

MARION: He's in his room.

JUSTER: Will dinner be at six?

MARION: I believe so. [JUSTER *exits left*]…I'm
sorry…

     FRANK *appears again.*

FRANK: Did you speak to me?

MARION: I'm sorry.

FRANK: You have broken my heart.

MARION: I saw you and I lost mine. And I also lost
my mind. That's why I followed you. I had lost my

mind. I thought of nothing but you. Each day I looked for you in the streets. And if not, I dreamt of you. A few days ago I looked outside this window and I thought I saw you moving among the trees. I thought I was hallucinating. This happened a few times. Were you there? Was that you?

FRANK: Yes.

MARION: What madness. It's my fault. I know it's my fault. I've been married since I was fifteen and I've never done anything like this. I love my husband and will always be faithful to him. I won't hurt him. He doesn't deserve this. Please, leave or I'll start crying and they will hear me and they will come and find me like this.

> *After a moment* FRANK *runs off.* MARION *goes to the couch and sits. She sobs. The lights fade. They come up again. The room is dimly lit.* JUSTER *enters.*

JUSTER: Have you been here all this time?

MARION: I was looking at the clouds. It seems it's going to rain.

> *He looks out.*

JUSTER: I don't think so. Night is falling. That's why it's getting dark. Dinner is served, dear. Will you come?

MARION: Yes...

JUSTER: Are you all right?

MARION: …No…I'm not feeling very well.

JUSTER: Should you have dinner?

MARION: …I don't think so…
    I'll go up to my room.

JUSTER: May I help you up?

MARION: I'll be up in a moment… [*He sits next to her*]
    What is today's date?

JUSTER: September twentieth.

MARION: Of course. It's the end of summer. The trees
    are beginning to turn.

JUSTER: Yes.

    She leans on his chest. He puts his arms around her.

MARION: Your hands are cold.

JUSTER: There is a change in the air.

    He strokes her hair.

Justin is only 1 who speaks of flowers

*~~the~~ Glazier takes his **vase** + drinks from it.*

ACT TWO

SCENE 17: *10th Street. Two years four months later. January, 1915. There is a telephone on the desk. It is early afternoon. The day is overcast.* MARION *stands by the window to the left. She looks out. She is motionless. An adagio is heard.*

SCENE 18: *10th Street. Three months later. April, 1915. It is late morning. A vase on the right stand is missing. A* GLAZIER *is standing on a ladder by the left window. He hammers points on the upper part of the window. He wears belted overalls.* MARION *enters right. She carries the vase with flowers. She stops to look at him. He continues working. She walks to the right stand. She looks at him again. She is transfixed. He turns to look at her. Their eyes lock. She cannot turn away.*

GLAZIER: Could I have a drink of water?

MARION: Yes.

She does not move. He comes halfway down the ladder and waits. Then he goes close to her, still looking at her. He puts the vase to his mouth

and drinks the water through the flowers. She
stares. He lets out a laugh. He looks at her.
GLAZIER: [*Referring to the water in the vase.*] May I?
   *He laughs again. She stares at him. She is pos-
   sessed. He takes flowers from the vase and puts
   them in her hair. He then picks her up and carries
   her upstage. They disappear behind the sofa. She
   emits a faint sound. The lights fade.*

SCENE 19: *10th Street. Five months later. September, 1915. It is evening.* MICHAEL *sits left.*
MARION *sits on the sofa. She looks pale and absent. She stares at the floor.* JUSTER *stands behind the sofa.*

JUSTER: I never thought I would have another child.
   I never thought Marion and I would have a child. I
   am so much older than she. I am beside myself with
   joy. Marion is a little worried. She is fearful. You
   are the first to know. I have suggested she ask Aunt
   Minnie to come and stay with us. Marion needs a
   woman's companionship. But she hasn't decided if
   she'll ask her. Maybe you could persuade her. She
   has missed you very much. I haven't heard any
   laughter in this house since you left. Marion has
   missed you. I hope you consider going to school in

New York this year. Marion is desolate, Michael.
Would you consider returning home?

> *Juster looks at* MARION. *He then looks at*
> MICHAEL *helplessly.* MICHAEL *looks at*
> MARION. *He is pained.*

MICHAEL: I will think about it, Father.

> SCENE 20: *10th Street. One year later. Septem-*
> *ber, 1916. It is late morning. Center stage, there is*
> *a rocking horse. On the horse there is a teddy bear.*
> MARION *enters from left. She carries* THOMAS,
> *eight months old. She takes the teddy bear.* FRANK
> *appears outside the window.*

FRANK: Hello.

MARION: ...Frank...

FRANK: My name is not Frank.

MARION: It isn't? [*He shakes his head*] What is your
name?

FRANK: Jonathan.

MARION: Jonathan?

FRANK: Yes.

MARION: Your name is not Frank? [*She laughs*] That's
not possible.

FRANK: My name is Jonathan. I was named after my
father.

> *She laughs.*

MARION: I'm so happy.

FRANK: Why?

MARION: I'm so glad to see you. [*She sighs*] Where have you been?

FRANK: I was away.

MARION: Where were you?

FRANK: In Michigan.

MARION: What were you doing in Michigan?

FRANK: Working with my uncle. Have you thought of me?

MARION: Oh, yes.

FRANK: What have you thought?

MARION: That I love you.

       Pause.

FRANK: What a pleasant surprise. [*Starting to step in.*] May I come in?

MARION: [*Laughing*] No.

FRANK: Come outside then.

MARION: Not now.

FRANK: When?

MARION: Tomorrow.

FRANK: At what time?

MARION: At one.

FRANK: Where?

MARION: In the square.

FRANK: Abingdon?

MARION: Yes.

FRANK: [*Moving his hand toward her*] See you then.

MARION: [*Her fingers touching his*] See you.

> SCENE 21: *10th Street. Five months later. February, 1917. It is evening.* MARION *sits to the left of the chess table.* MICHAEL *sits down right.*

MARION: He often speaks of closing the house and moving south, where the weather is temperate. He likes using that word. Temperate. It's quite clear why he does. He means moral balance. Evenness of character. He means that he knows what I do when I leave the house. That he knows about Frank and me. He's saying that he'll seek moderation at any cost. That he's ready to divorce me and put an end to our family life. I'm ready for it. I'm ready to face him with it. He's just making it easier for me. [MICHAEL *looks down*] What's the matter?

MICHAEL: When I'm with him, I care about nothing but him. [*They look at each other for a moment*] I love him. He's my father and I love him. And I don't want to see him suffer. When I'm with you I forget that he's my father and I take your side. He's my father and I love him and I respect him. And I feel terrible that I've been disloyal to him. And I feel worse to see that he's still gentle and kind to both you and me. I'm sorry because I love you too, and I know that you too need me. But I can't bear being divided, and I have to choose him. I'm leaving, Marion. I can't remain here any longer knowing what I know and feeling as I do about it. It's too painful and I'm demeaned by my betrayal of him. There are times when I want to tell him the whole truth. And if I don't, it's because I love you too and I feel there's no wrong in what you're doing. I really don't. I think you're right in what you're doing. You're young and you're in love and it's a person's right to love. I think so. Frank is handsome and I think he is honest. I mean, I think he loves you. He's not very strong, but he's young. No one is strong when he is young. I'm not. Only I'm still playing with soldiers and he has entered into the grown-up world. If I were in his place it would terrify me to be the lover of a married woman. Good-bye, my sister. I must leave. I am constantly forced to act in a cowardly manner. I cannot be loyal to both, and I cannot choose one over the other, and I feel a coward when I look at you, and I feel a coward when I look at him. I am tearing out my heart and leaving it here, as half of it is yours, and the other half is his. I hope I won't hurt you by leaving—beyond missing me, which I know you will. I mean beyond that. I mean that I hope my leaving has no consequences beyond our missing each other. Take care. [*He starts to go, then turns*] What if you're discovered? Will he get a job, take on such responsibility? Will he marry you?

MARION: ...I don't know. I haven't thought about that...

JUSTER: [*Offstage right, in a disconnected manner*] Are you leaving? [*A short pause*] Are you staying for dinner?

MICHAEL: I have some studying to do.

JUSTER: [*Offstage*] Stay. We should be eating soon. You could leave after dinner. We should have dinner soon. [*He enters and walks to center with a glazed look. He stops, still facing left, and looks at the floor as he speaks.*] How are you, my dear?

MARION: ...Good evening...

JUSTER: You both look somber. I hope nothing's wrong.

MARION: ...No, nothing's wrong.

JUSTER: [*Walking left as he speaks*] I've had a bad day myself. Sit down, Michael. I'll be back in a moment. [*The volume of his voice does not change as he leaves the room*] I'll he back in a moment. [*There is the sound of water running as he washes his hands*] It was difficult at work today. Everyone seems to be constantly shirking responsibility. That seems to be the main problem in the world today. It's not possible to get things done properly, both in the house and at work. Will the person whose duty it is to prepare dinner be here on time to prepare it? Will that person be at the market early enough to ensure that the ingredients he gets are fresh and not wilted and sour? [*He enters drying his hands with a hand towel*] Will my office staff appear to work properly dressed and properly shaven? It seems as if each day the lesson has to be taught again. The same lesson. Each day we have to restore mankind to a civilized state. Each night the savage takes over. We're entering the war. I'm sure we are. In no time we will be in the middle of a war. Yes, you wash your face! Yes, you comb your hair. Yes, you wear clothes that are not soiled. Why can't people understand that if something is worth doing it's worth doing right! [*He sits down and puts the towel on his lap with meticulous care. He takes one of his shoes off*] I take care of my feet. My socks are in a good state of repair. When they wear out I pass them on to someone who needs them. [*Taking off his other shoe*] Others mend their socks. I don't. I don't mind wearing mended clothes. My underwear is mended. So are my shirts, but not my socks. [*With both

47

feet on the floor] I have always wanted to give my feet the maximum of comfort. It is they who support the whole body yet they are fragile. Feet are small and fragile for the load they carry. I wear stockings that fit so they won't fold and create discomfort to my feet. If I treat my feet with respect, my brain functions with respect. It functions with more clarity and so does my stomach. I digest better. In the morning at the office, I look at my mail. Then I call my assistant. I discuss some matters with him. Then I call my secretary. She comes in with her stenographer's pad and sits down on the chair to my right. I collect my thoughts for a few moments. [*Standing*] Then I stand on my feet, walk to the window at my left, and from there, standing on my feet with my stomach properly digesting my breakfast and my brain as clear as the morning dew, I dictate my letters.

MARION: I will go see if dinner is ready. [*She exits left*]

JUSTER: What is wrong with Marion? She's not herself.

MICHAEL: Nothing. Nothing I know of.

JUSTER: What is wrong with you? What is the matter with you?

MICHAEL: Nothing, Father.

JUSTER: Have you thought it over?

MICHAEL: What?

JUSTER: Are you coming home?

MICHAEL: Not yet.

> JUSTER *sits.*

JUSTER: Fine. You do as you must, Michael. [*There is a pause*] It is hard to know whom to trust, whom to show your heart to.

> *He picks up his shoes and puts them on his lap.*

MARION: [*Offstage*] Dinner is ready.

JUSTER: Come, Michael.

> MICHAEL *walks up to* JUSTER *and waits for him.* JUSTER *is still sitting.*

Let's have dinner.

SCENE 22: *10th Street. Two weeks later. March, 1917. It is late afternoon.* MARION *and* FRANK *are embracing in the space behind the sofa. She speaks with urgency.*

MARION: I have been warned that this is a dream. That tomorrow you won't love me. I've been told I must prepare myself. That when you leave me my life will end. That my pain will be eternal. Hold me. Hold me in your arms. [*He does*] Something terrible is happening. Something terrible happens each day. You're not touched by it—but I am impure. I lie and lie each day, every minute, every hour. I am

49

rotten and deceitful. Except to you, each time I speak I tell a lie. I am deceitful. I am impure. How I wish I could spend my days with you, only with you and with no one else. And to speak only the truth…only the truth…only the truth. [*There is a pause*] Frank, wouldn't you like it if we spent all our time together, day and night? If we traveled together? If we walked on the street together, holding hands? If we spent our evenings together sleeping in each other's arms? How would you like that? [*There is a silence*] Frank…

FRANK: We have to be careful.

SCENE 23: *10th Street. Two weeks later. Evening.* MARION *sits at the desk and prepares to write.* JUSTER *enters from the garden. He looks at her for a while. Then he walks quietly to her side. He caresses her hair, then tightens his fist around it. She lets out a whimper. He holds onto her hair, then releases it. She is frightened and motionless. He stares at her for a while longer. He then takes a paper from his pocket and puts it on the desk. She looks at it, lowers her eyes and remains motionless.*

JUSTER: [*Threateningly*] Do you know what this is? [*She looks away*] What is it? [*Pause*] Tell me!

MARION: [*In a deadened tone*] A receipt.

JUSTER: For what? [*Pause*] For what?

MARION: For an apartment.

JUSTER: For what purpose? [*Pause*] For what purpose?

> *She starts to rise. He puts his hands on her shoulders, forces her to sit, and continues to put pressure on her.*

JUSTER: [*In a quiet, controlled voice*] What have you done? [*Pause*] What have you done?

> *They look at each other. She is unflinching. He puts pressure on her shoulders until she falls to the floor. He takes a chair and raises it over his head to hit her. She screams. He stops himself. He puts the chair down and exits left. She rises slowly, goes to the left window and looks.* FRANK *enters from the right. She turns to him. She is confused. They walk to each other. She starts to gesture towards the garden nervously. He takes her hand. She starts to pull it away.* JUSTER *enters the garden. She looks towards the garden.* JUSTER *goes to the window and looks in.* JUSTER *looks at them. The lights begin to dim.*

SCENE 24: *10th Street. A few hours later.* JUSTER *sits at the desk. He opens the drawers, takes out letters, deeds, notebooks, address books, checkbooks, photographs, documents, and ledgers and arranges them on top of the desk rapidly.*

JUSTER's *briefcase is on the floor, next to the desk.* MARION *enters. She stands left.* JUSTER *ignores* MARION *and takes out a few more papers.*

JUSTER: What are your plans?

MARION: In regard to what?

JUSTER: In regard to your life!

MARION: I've not made any plans.

JUSTER: Well, do. I'd like to know what you intend to do. How soon can you decide? I want to know what you plan to do as soon as possible. [*He places the briefcase on his lap and puts the papers in the briefcase as he speaks*] I expect you to leave as soon as possible. I expect you to move your things—what you can, today. A few things. What you need for immediate use. The rest I'll have sent to the place you choose. If you have a place of your own, you should move there. [*She starts to speak. He continues*] Thomas will stay with me. [*She starts to go.*] Don't bother to look for him. Don't think you're taking him with you. You waste your time looking for him. He's not in the house. I have taken him to a place where you won't find him and no one but I knows where that is. So don't bother to look for him. [MARION *reenters*] I am leaving now. I'll return later tonight. When I return I expect you'll be gone. Jennie will help you pack and she will take you and whatever things you want to that place or any other place you wish. If you don't leave, you'll never see Thomas. You're an adulterous wife and I'll sue you for divorce. A court will grant me sole custody of the child. Do you have anything to say?

There is a moment's silence.

MARION: I will not leave unless I take Thomas with me.

JUSTER: If you're still here when I return, you'll never see him again.

MICHAEL *enters right.* JUSTER *speaks to him.*

JUSTER: Marion is leaving tonight and she'll never enter this house again. She's not wanted here. She has debased this house. She will not be forgiven and her name will never be mentioned here again. And if you think of her ever again you'll never enter this house.

MICHAEL: Father, may I intercede?

JUSTER: In regard to what!

MICHAEL: Father—

JUSTER: [*Interrupting*] No. I will not hear what you have to say. I don't want your advice. Marion will leave. You may escort her wherever it is she is going if you wish.

SCENE 25: MARY's *place. Two months later. May, 1917. It is evening.* MARY *sits on the sofa.* JUSTER *sits left. He wears a hat and coat and holds his briefcase on his lap.*

JUSTER: I never saw myself as deserving of her love. She was preciously beautiful, modest. She was thoughtful and respectful. There was no vanity in her. When her mother died I don't believe she cried once but her spirit left her. She seemed absent. This was the way she grieved. She was obedient. She did what was asked of her, but she had lost her sense of judgment and her desire to choose one thing over the other. She accepted what others chose for her. She sat for hours staring into space. I took her for walks. I took her to the park. We took boat rides. Our meetings became more frequent. We were natural companions. I loved her company, and I found myself always thinking of her. She was sad and still when I wasn't there. When she saw me, she smiled and came to life. Her aunt told me this too. That she only smiled when she saw me. I foolishly believed that this meant she loved me. I proposed marriage and she accepted. Her aunt, too, thought it natural when I asked for her hand in marriage. She gave us her blessings. There was no exuberant joy in our wedding, but there was the most profound tenderness. I was very happy and I thought Marion was also. There were times when

she was taciturn, but I thought she was still griev-
ing for her mother. She was a child and she needed
a mother more than a husband. But a husband is
all she had. I could not be a mother to her. Seven
years later Marion had a child. I was overwhelmed
with joy, but Marion was not. She became more
taciturn than ever. [*There is a pause*] I began to feel
she hated me. And she does hate me, and she has
made me hate her. You see her. I know you see her.
I know you go to that apartment frequently. I've
seen you go in. [*Pause*] Tell me, Mary, what is she
like with him? [*Pause*] War has been declared, and
I'm afraid that Michael will be drafted. He, too, will
be taken away from me.

SCENE 26: *Abingdon Square. Two weeks later.
June, 1917. It is evening.* MARION *stands left.*
MARY *sits right. They drink vermouth and smoke.*
MARION: I am in a state of despair! Thanks to Frank.
How could I not be? [*Turning to* MARY] Why did
you do that? [*To* MARY] Have you ever lived with
someone who speaks one way and acts another!
Someone for whom words mean nothing? Or if
they mean anything, they mean something different
from what they mean to you? My life is a puzzle. I
don't know where I stand. I am constantly asking:

55

What do you mean? What is it you mean? What does that mean to you? Why did you say that? Why did you do that? Have you?

MARY: Me?

MARION *sits left.*

MARION: When I sinned against life because I was dead I was not punished. Now that life has come unto me I am destroyed and I destroy everything around me. May God save me. I have always trusted in his goodness and his divine understanding. May God have mercy on me. I have never denied him.

SCENE 27: *A beer parlor. Two weeks later. Evening. A square table.* JUSTER *sits left.* MICHAEL *sits right. There is a glass of beer in front of each.* JUSTER *speaks obsessively.*

JUSTER: I have tried. I offered her some money. She didn't accept it. I knew she wouldn't. She stared at me and said nothing. We were in a public place. She stared and I waited for her to answer. After a while I knew she had no intention of answering. I said to her, "Do you have anything to say?" She still said nothing but I felt the hatred in her eyes. I said, "I suppose you are not accepting my offer?" She said nothing. I said, "For God's sake, say whether you don't accept it or not and if you don't let's get on to something else." Her hatred is such, it burns. Paper would burn if it were held up to her glance. When I reached the door I saw her back reflected in the glass. She was so still that there was no life in her. She was still like a dead person. I regretted having offered her the money. I had no reason to think she would accept it. What do they live on. [*Short pause*] Have you seen her?

MICHAEL: No.

JUSTER: She's gone berserk. She is wild like a mad woman. She's insane. You haven't seen her?

MICHAEL: No.

JUSTER: You haven't been in touch at all? Letters?

MICHAEL: No.

JUSTER: Last week I followed her to a dance parlor. [MICHAEL *looks at him*] Yes, Michael. You have not been here and you don't realize what's going on. Marion's behavior is irrational. She's not sane. I followed her and she went in a dance parlor. It was still light outside, and yet people were already dancing. I followed her in and I took a table by the window. A man wearing a soldier's uniform greeted her. They started dancing. And moved to a dark corner. She knew I was there looking at her and that's why she did what she did. They kissed and caressed lewdly. I've never seen such behavior in public. Never did I think I would see someone…I so cherished behave like that. She knew I was there. She knew I could see them, and yet she did what she did. [*He takes a drink*] One day, last week, she came to my office. I was standing by the window. I did not notice her at first. Then I heard her say, "Does this happen every afternoon?" I turned to her. She had been standing at the door. And I said "Does what happen every afternoon?" She said, "Do you stand at the window every afternoon?" I said, "Yes." And she said, "What do you look at?" I said, "I look out. I don't look at anything in particular. I look out because that's how I concentrate on what I have to do." "And what is it you have to do?" "Right now I'm in the middle of dictating my letters." Then she stood behind my secretary and leaned over to look at her writing pad. Then she said, "What is that? A secret code?" Shorthand! Then she came to where I was. She said to me, "That is a love letter." She then looked out the window and said, "Do you use binoculars?" I told her that I could see quite well without binoculars and she said, "From where you are, can you see the house on Abingdon Square? Can you see it? Can you see it?" She thought I was spying on her. She's mad. She's capable of anything. [*He looks absently as he takes a revolver from his pocket and puts it on the table*] I carry this with me at all times. I don't know if I will shoot her or if I will shoot myself. I know one of us will die soon.

MICHAEL: ...Father...I must try to stop you.

JUSTER *puts the revolver in his pocket. He takes a purse out of his pocket, takes money out and puts it on the table. He stands and starts to walk away. He stops.*

JUSTER: Would you take care of the bill, Michael?

MICHAEL: ...Yes...[JUSTER *starts to exit*] Father... I've enlisted.

JUSTER *stops, looks at* MICHAEL *for a moment, turns away slowly and exits.*

SCENE 28: *Abingdon Square. Two weeks later. July, 1917.* MARION *stands up left.* MARY *sits right.*

MARY: Who? Juster?

MARION: Yes, Juster. I hate him. I will shoot him. I imagine I shoot him and I feel a great satisfaction. A satisfaction equal to flushing a toilet, seeing the water flush out and vanish forever. I am crude. I know I'm crude. I know I'm uncivilized. I know I am a part of a civilized race but I am uncivilized. Thomas is not his!

MARY: Marion!

MARION: He's not.

MARY: Is he Frank's?

MARION: No.

MARY: Whose is he?

MARION: [*She lets out a loud laugh.*] A stranger's. A stranger. Just someone. Someone who came in the house one day and never again. I never saw him again. Just a man. A stranger. No one. I have a bad destiny, Mary. I have an evil destiny. It constantly thwarts me. Nothing comes to me at the right time or in the right way.

> SCENE 29: MINNIE's *living room. One week later. It is evening.* MINNIE *sits on a chair, center stage.* MARION *is on her knees facing* MINNIE.

MARION: I need my child. I need my child, Minnie. I need that child in my arms and I don't see a way I could ever have him again. He has been irrevocably taken from me. There is nothing I could do that would bring him back to me. I have begged him to let me see him. I have gone on my knees, I have offered myself to him. I have offered my life to him. He won't listen to me. He won't forgive me. I'm at his mercy. I wish for his death. I stalk the house. I stand on the corner and I watch the house. I imagine the child inside playing in his room. When spring comes I may be able to see him in the garden. I know he's not there, but that's how I can feel him near me. Stalking the house.

MINNIE: Why won't he let you see him?

MARION: He's gone mad! He's insane, Minnie.

MINNIE: Juster?

MARION: Yes! He's insane! He wants to destroy me. But I'll destroy him first.

MINNIE: Marion, I don't understand you. I forget things. I'm too old. I don't remember what you're talking about. It's no longer in my mind. [*Touching the side of her head*] The flesh is sore and swollen. This part of it is stretched and redder than the rest, as if it's hotter. As if it had a fever. As if it had hair. It throbs.

SCENE 30: *10th Street. A few days later. It is late morning.* JUSTER *sits at the desk. He speaks to* MICHAEL *on the phone. After a few moments* MARION *appears outside the left window. She is spying on* JUSTER.

JUSTER: She follows me. She's insane. She's jealous, Michael. She is jealous of me. Her jealousy is irrational. As irrational as everything else she does.

MARION *makes a move and makes a noise.* JUSTER *turns toward her.*

JUSTER: [*To* MARION] What are you doing?

MARION: Who is here with you?

JUSTER: I'm alone. I'm talking on the telephone.

> *She hears a sound and turns to the left.*

MARION: What was that? Someone's in the back.

> *She exits left. He speaks to* MICHAEL.

JUSTER: She is outside. Doing who knows what in the garden. She just looked through the window and demanded to know who is here with me. There is no one here with me. Not even Jenny is here. I have sent her away. I prefer to be alone.

> MARION *enters right.*

MARION: Who are you with?

JUSTER: I am with no one.

MARION: Who are you talking to?

JUSTER: I'm talking on the telephone. [*She takes the receiver from him, listens for a moment, shakes the receiver, blows on the mouthpiece, and hangs up. She walks around the room.*]

MARION: I love this house. I had forgotten how I loved this house. [*Pause*] I have been ill. I have had fevers. [*Pause*] I'll tell you a riddle. See if you can solve it:

If a person owns an object, where is it? It's under his arm.

If a person loves an object, where is it? It's in his arms.

If a mother's baby is not in her arms, where is it?
[*Pause*] Where is it? Where is Thomas? Where
have you taken him? Is there someone in your life?
Someone influencing you? How can you do this?
How can you put me through this? What do you gain?

SCENE 31: *Abingdon Square. Two weeks later. Au-*
gust, 1917. It is evening. The stage is dark. There is
the sound of a gunshot. The lights come up.
JUSTER *stands downstage facing up. He wears*
an overcoat and a bowler hat. His right arm hangs,
holding a revolver. MARION *is up center. She faces*
him. Her arms are halfway raised and her mouth
and eyes are open in a state of shock. MARY *en-*
ters running from the left. MARION *turns to look*
at MARY. *Both* JUSTER *and* MARION *go through*
the motions he describes.

JUSTER: I came in. I said nothing. I took the gun out
and aimed at her. She stared at me. Her courage is
true. She stared at death without flinching. My eye
fell on the mirror behind her. I saw my reflection
in it. I am much older than she. Much older. I
looked very old and she looked very young. I felt
ashamed to love her so. I thought, "Let her young
lover kill her if she must die." I turned the gun to
my head. She moved toward me calmly. She put

her hand on mine and brought it down away from my head. She said, "Please." I was moved by her kindness. I turned to look at her. And again I was filled with rage. My finger pulled the trigger.

He shoots again. MARION *screams, runs upstage and returns to her position at the start of the scene.*

JUSTER: That was the blast you heard. The gun was aiming at the floor. Everyone here is perfectly all right.

JUSTER *begins to choke. It is a stroke. He turns front slowly. He starts to walk backwards gasping for air. He falls unconscious on the sofa. His eyes are wide open.*

SCENE 32: *10th Street. A month later. September, 1917. It is dusk.* FRANK *stands behind the couch to the left.* MARION *sits right of the couch. She is serene and composed.*

FRANK: And if he doesn't come to, will you spend the rest of your life taking care of him?

MARION: When I reach out to touch him I don't know if I'm reaching outside of me or into me. If he doesn't come out of the coma...? I feed him. I bathe him. I change him. I wait for the day when I can speak to him...speak to him at least once.

FRANK: I wanted to ask you if there is anything I can do.

MARION: ... No.... Thank you, Frank.

FRANK sits on the right side of the couch.

FRANK: I may be leaving once again, Marion.

MARION: Oh…?

FRANK: Yes, I may be moving on.

MARION: I know, Frank. I know you must go.

They sit silently for a while.

SCENE 33: JUSTER's *bedroom. A day later. It is evening.* JUSTER *lies in his bed unconscious. He is in a coma. He is unshaven.* MARION *stands on the upstage side of the bed.* JUSTER *begins to come to. His speech is impaired.*

JUSTER: …It looks much nicer here than in the parlor…

MARION: What does?

JUSTER: …It feels bad.

MARION: What feels bad?

JUSTER: …It is happier here…

MARION: What?

JUSTER: It's happier. Don't you know it.

MARION: What?

His eyes open.

JUSTER: Who's here.

MARION: It's me.

JUSTER: Who?

MARION: Marion.

JUSTER: Marion?

MARION: Yes.

JUSTER: Why are you here?

MARION: Because you're ill.

JUSTER: What's wrong with me?

MARION: You had a stroke.

JUSTER: What have you done to me!

MARION: Nothing.

JUSTER: Yes, you have.

MARION: What have I done?

JUSTER: You've done harm to me.

MARION: No.

He looks at her suspiciously.

JUSTER: What have you done to me? Get out!

MARION: I've nursed you. I've fed you.

JUSTER: What have you fed me?

She is silent.

Poison!

MARION: No.

JUSTER: I hate you! You're repulsive to me! [*Pause*] You've touched me!

MARION: Yes.

JUSTER: Do you enjoy seeing me like this! [*Pause*] Where's Michael? [*Pause*] Has he been here?

MARION: I sent for him.

JUSTER: I want to see him.

MARION: He's trying to get here.

JUSTER: Why can't he come?

MARION: They won't give him leave.

JUSTER: [*Starting to get out of bed*] I want to get up. [*During the following lines, he tries to get up and she tries to stop him.*] I want to be downstairs when he calls.

MARION: He won't call till later.

JUSTER: I'll call him.

MARION: He can't be reached.

> *He collapses.*

JUSTER: Am I dying?

MARION: ...I don't know.

> *He tries to get up.*

JUSTER: I don't want you here. [*She takes a step back*] Get out! Get out! [*She starts to leave, then stops*] Get out!

MARION: ...May I come back later? [*He does not answer*] I understand.

> *She exits. He lifts himself to a sitting position, stands and stumbles to the living room.*

JUSTER: ... Marion.... Marion! [*He starts to fall*] ...Marion... [*He crawls*] Marion...Marion...

> MARION *runs in. She holds* JUSTER *in her arms.*

JUSTER: I love you.

MARION: …I love you too.

She sobs. MICHAEL *enters, walks to them, and stands behind them. He wears an army uniform. There is a shaft of light behind them. As* MARION *speaks,* JUSTER's *hand begins to rise.*

MARION: Michael…! Michael…! He mustn't die! He mustn't die! Don't die…! Don't die…!

His hand touches her face.

MARION: …He'll be all right. He'll be all right.

END OF PLAY

GREEN INTEGER
Pataphysics and Pedantry

Edited by Per Bregne
Douglas Messerli, *Publisher*

Essays, Manifestos, Statements, Speeches, Maxims,
Epistles, Diaristic Notes, Narratives, Natural Histories,
Poems, Plays, Performances, Ramblings, Revelations
and all such ephemera as may appear necessary
to bring society into a slight tremolo of confusion
and fright at least.

*

Green Integer Books

BOOKS FORTHCOMING FROM GREEN INTEGER